Uniform

Uniform

Poems by

Lisa Stice

Kelsay Books

Cover art: *Une Spartiate Donnant un Bouclier à son Fils*
(Spartan Woman Giving a Shield to Her Son)
Jean-Jacques-François Le Barbier, 1805

ISBN 13:978-0692667019

Kelsay Books
Aldrich Press
www.kelsaybooks.com

For Saoirse and Seamus

Acknowledgments

Thank you to my parents and brother for your love and continuous support. Thank you to Jesse for supporting me in writing about this topic and for giving me commentary on my poems even when you were thousands of miles away. Thank you to Saoirse for being a good napper and for sometimes listening to poetry collections in place of bedtime stories. Thank you to Seamus for being content with lying by my feet while I typed at the computer. Thank you to Anne Caston for your rigorous expectations, to Zack Rogow for teaching me the power of revision, to Linda McCarriston for inspiring fearlessness, and to Elizabeth Bradfield for encouraging risk and for instilling confidence.

I am grateful to the editors of the following literary magazines in which some of these poems first appeared, some in slightly different versions: "Brides and Grooms" *On the Rusk* volume 6, issue 7, "In Training" *Inklette* issue 1, "Family Code" *The Birds We Piled Loosely* issue 6, "Long Distance" *Riding Light* volume 2, issue 3, "Unconventional Warfare" *Inklette* issue 2, "The Night before Deployment" *o-Dark-Thirty: The Review* vol 4, issue 3.

Contents

Introduction   13

I

Wedding Arch   17
On Duty   18
Unconventional Warfare   19
Lejeune's Resolution   20
Esprit de Corps at Home   21
Watching the Birthday Moto Video   23
Dress Code   24
Memo to the Wives   25
In Training   26
Duty Stations   27
Labor Days   28
Concerning Politics   29
Family Day   30
Uniform   31
An Officer's Wife   32

II

While in Uniform   37
Deployment Notices   38
For Efficiency   40
Spartan Wives   41
Family Readiness   42
The Night before Deployment   43
Law   44
Geometry of Fire on the Local News   46
The Pit Opened Up   47
Hush-a-Bye   48

1st   49
Traditions   50
Concerning Social Media   51
Cemetery   53
A Funeral for Our Own   55
Penelope   56
Long Distance   57
Corps Value   58
Range Operations   59
Family Code   60

III

Deployment Coming to a Close   63
At Play   64
The Amazons Prepare for Retrograde 65
How Foolishly He Had Acted   66
Retrograde   68
Group Meetings   69
Continued Operations   70
A Dependable Order   71
Posthumously   72
Widows Receive a Free Ticket
    to the Birthday Ball   73
3rd Anniversary   75
Words from Friends   76
Irregular   77
Between Trainings and Deployments 78
Brides and Grooms   79

Notes on the Poems
About the Author

Introduction

I am married to the Marine Corps. It's quite a different sort of marriage than the one with my husband, who was already a Marine when we married. My husband and I talk and compromise when we disagree or are making plans that would impact both of us; my husband and I speak up when the other hurts us or makes us upset. The Corps culture promotes silence and leaves little to no room for compromise. I understand that some silences are justified within the Corps, like not disclosing where and when my husband will deploy because that information in the wrong hands puts many lives in danger. Other silences I do not understand. For Marines and their families, speaking up about frustrations is viewed as unsupportive and, sometimes, as unpatriotic. My husband can even face consequences for my speaking up.

I would like to begin the long-needed conversation…

I

The Marine Corps ought not to permit marriage.
A monastic order, all the way. Married men
make poor soldiers. If the government
wanted you to have a wife, they'd issue you one.

—LtGen Lewis B. "Chesty" Puller, USMC

Wedding Arch

Kiss for permission to pass underneath
etched Mameluke blades raised and lowered
and raised again.

Pass, uniformed in tradition,
between the lines of men
who cannot kiss their wives this day.

Press his cold medals against
your collar bone and
smile though he will be gone

nine months from now.
Wish you could have held
that kiss a little longer

before the final blade
strikes your backside
and you are formally initiated.

On Duty

walk on your Marine's left side

the protected place
opposite the theoretical sword

you may hold his left hand
if he's not in uniform

be thankful to walk by his side
be content with no happily-ever-after plots

in 0100 homecomings
laundry loads of PT gear

leaving interim friends
to start again in another state

be his shining medal
always faithful

to love all things holy
in this sacred institution

be respectful and kind
in your wooden fearlessness

Unconventional Warfare

When the wooden horse rolled in
and its side fell open, you braced,
stiffened your muscles, but
no assault, only darkness
with a promise of surprise—
so you waited. Sometimes
you climbed up its flank and neck
looked into its eye's cavern
and held your breath. It followed
on its ancient casters with creaky
warnings at the commissary,
the family readiness meeting,
the ring of your land line.
It followed you to the officers' BBQ
and its wooden jaws cracked open
She's no moto wife. She doesn't
even run. Her dog is just a tiny, little thing.
She doesn't plan to join the softball team,
and you saw the other wives
cordoned off inside the beast's belly,
and your husband ate ribs and laughed.

Lejeune's Resolution

commemorating the birth of the Marine Corps
10 November, 1775

since that date
many thousands borne
in memory

the Corps bears
glories of its record
a footprint in history

in action
honors in war
tranquility at home

generation after generation
gray in war
in peace and security

birth
honors
virtue

this high name
this eternal spirit
in every age

equal to every past

worthy successors
the long line of men

Esprit de Corps at Home

the choice
you had in mind

the specific question
the representation of

disturbed thought
brought to your attention

such representation
an integral part

of the already represented
point of view

in passing
in amending

consider the question
provide for it

your feeling
renewed representation

inspired by individuals
who raised the flag

who placed folded flags on mantels

this feeling

profoundly aware of
the many deeds

of knuckles white in prayer
of duty's call from within

combat spirit
assumed conviction

organization for support
for emergency

readiness
provision

combined for service
in defense

may be essential
may be assigned

many times in our history
again

Watching the Birthday Moto Video

Ooh-rah! from the Marines.
Moto even here,
moto to the end.

But the ones, ringed, who love them
do not want them
to be moto stars

or purple hearts that return
and return
and return
to volunteer for desert fire.

So we hesitate to answer
the knock on the door
the unexpected phone call,

but gold stars expect adherence
from the grunting men
who are *always faithful*.

Dress Code

Wear a dress or business casual pants and top
for change-of-command or retirement ceremonies.

Crisp pants or skirt and modest blouse
for dinners and holiday functions.

On or off base your Marine is responsible for you—
Absolutely with no equivocation:

Nice shirts, khakis, modest shorts, un-ripped jeans
for personal and all other daily events.

Tea or full-length gowns for formal occasions,
no slit slip dresses, uncomely color combinations,

too tight dresses, or revealing cuts.
You are part of the few and the proud. Think

about your husband when dressing.
Plenty of events, rules.

Backlash varies command to command,
from all-night stares to formal follow-up.

You don't want your husband reprimanded
for something you could have prevented.

Memo to the Wives

we need your help
worthwhile opportunities open to all
please see our flyer
contact us for more information

please join us for a brief presentation
opportunities for Q
&A if answers permit
childcare will not be provided

be on lookout for the perfect
you seem accepting, proper
        only required of volunteers
sign up on our volunteer list
your committed duty

In Training

While   you   are away
(somewhere)   training—
   7 killed   an accident   mechanical failure
   over water   then into   the water   an accident
                        debris   and   remains
   washed onto the beach   not identified

                                        where are you?

                    4 killed   an accident
   live ammunition   mortars
   grenades
4 sweep the field   1 undetonated mortar
      found

            undetonated until   found

                                        where are you?

                    tanks on the beach   stumble upon

         by accident   when running   an
accident

                                        where

                                           are

                                              you?

26

Duty Stations

assigned
transferred
served this tour
relief operations
subsequently assigned
served
assumed command
in support of command
a joint tour
responsible for command
deployed
then transferred
currently assigned
gold star leadership
there and there and here

Labor Days

I wish we could accommodate you,
but we're understaffed
and no beds are available.

My second day of
throwing up water
and not sleeping.

We'd have to admit you
to treat your dehydration, but
contractions need to be 1 minute apart.

Through worry
and exhaustion
my dog lies curled on my hip.

Concerning Politics

review imposed campaigning restrictions
avoid any inference of approval or disapproval
sponsorship or endorsement implied
or appearance of partisan politics

no campaigning for partisan candidates
no fundraising activities or canvasing
no service in clubs or speeches at gatherings
no uniforms when acting as spectator

partisan posters and signs should not
be visible to the public at your residence
take care not to post or link material
with opinions about public officials

but you may vote for whomever you choose

Family Day

Chicken and potato salad
provided by
the First ***** Church
water donated by
***** Credit Union

bring your own lawn chairs

activities for children:
photo copied coloring book pages
bins of broken crayons
face painting by volunteer moms
the executive officer
dressed as Santa

bring your cameras

gift for each child
(generous donations
of various businesses)
attendance not mandatory
but expected
whether you have dependants
or not

Uniform

slight changes
the last such changes
for some time at least
directed by higher authority

a new cover
with a broader brim
for combat
action well-fitted

affix eagle-globe-and-anchor
emblem of respect
of commitment

adopt the new pattern
of ideals
in a timely manner

combat swagger
feel the need of it
place it in a box
until

An Officer's Wife

comes with privilege
and corresponding obligation
directives, procedures, attendance checks
anxiety of non-acceptance

learns not to ask *what did you do today*
security of sensitive information
sound judgment when ordering a drink
when driving on base

when discussing current events
discretion failed will be dealt with
promptly, and with sufficient severity
to the attention of higher authority

Who are you? he asked.
I counted chevrons on his sleeve
and answered *A wife.*
Who are you? he ordered.
Someone who needs
access to the other side of the gate.

II

Come on, you sons of bitches! Do you want to live forever?

—SgtMaj Daniel J. "Dan" Daley, USMC

While in Uniform

          Your cover
pulled low   hides
                              your eyes
            no kiss
                  no hug
we say
        good bye

Deployment Notices

While your husband's away,
just let me know when you need help.

Trash bag hanging from my wrist,
I push a stroller across the complex
to the dumpster; neighbors pass or
watch from their balcony doors.

Some time we'll have to
have you over for dinner.

I have become skilled
at meals for one,
and sometimes leftovers
taste pretty good.

The next time I see you,
I'll give you my number just in case.

If the woman on the corner
is already outside
when I walk by with the dog and baby,
she steps behind her patio tree.

The Coping During Deployment Meeting
is cancelled, no replacement date.

It's been five months,

and my body has grown accustomed
to four hours of sleep so I can give
the baby and dog what they need.

For Efficiency

personally responsible
thoughts
his duty
to standard
on the part of all
the good name
power of example
from gentlemen raised
held by the people
tempered with discipline
appearance of
neatly dressed
appearance of
courtesy
military salutes
courtesy

in these letters
concern
to the Corps
a strict duty
you are the Corps
esprit in your hands
the young take their cue
on reputation
kindly and just
regulations
enacted uniform
in a military manner
a compliance
discipline
discipline
salute

Spartan Wives

assume every great burden

of home and hearth and land
of balancing accounts
of mowing lawns
of pursuing degrees

moulded

for courage to change
to leave the house
even if his call might go missed
always ready
always willing

to keep complaints in journals
keep
confidence that
women merit trust
survive an empty return

Family Readiness

The paper pocket-folder
you left for me
in the file drawer of our desk:
limited power of attorney
your social security number
logins and passwords
names of command I can't call
because they are with you
your deployment address blank
our bank accounts
contacts for your relatives
chaplain's email
(but he'll be gone too)
family birth certificates
list of what you want buried with you
how you'd want to be dressed
the song you'd want played
just in case

The Night before Deployment

I say, *I need you to come back*
but you are asleep.
I think of the flak vest and helmet,
jump and dive gear,
weighted rucksacks
stacked in the living room.

I should have faith
in the Corpsman's vigilance,
in sound training,
in your drown proofing,
in your combat drills,

but where was my training?
I think of the tasks unfinished,
a toy box held together with clamps,
sockets without safety plugs,
cabinets and drawers free to open—
our daughter will crawl and walk

in the months you are gone,
and I need to protect her.

Law

be it enacted
as the President directs
a proper distribution of rank
a company
a detachment of order

be it further enacted
that all will pay
the subsistence
of flexibility at home
of birthdays and burials

be it further enacted
that Corps of Marines
respective dependants
detached
from time to time

be it further enacted
the same oath
the same rules
established and employed
the same allowance

be it further enacted
into service
of who you are
and will be

in debt and contract

be it further enacted
by these actions
at any time liable
to duty in the garrisons
or on any shore

Geometry of Fire on the Local News

Smoke swells in its climb
and crawl beyond the hills—
a controlled burn,
now out of control.

Twister flames feed
themselves and grow—
now consuming self
as fire battles

dry brush just outside
the maneuver range.
Marines continue
to train. They cough

from the choke of smoke—
even creosote ash and scorch
cannot persuade tears.

The Pit Opened Up

Past years made us weary
It would take much
to draw them into another war
but troops were deployed
over wide swaths of land
forces built up
relieving the besieged towns
a series of tactical conflicts
fieldcraft and marksmanship

Where are you?
I imagine you
seven stars in your right hand
Can you bear them?
In your other hand
a little book   open

Some people like to go far away
I am home
the roadbed is almost ready to be surfaced
children go to school
there is silence of half an hour
I must remember
to make an appointment with the dentist

Hush-a-Bye

26 miles away
Marines play drums:
missiles and mortars.
My heart,
my daughter's breath,
our rocking
fall in with the
cadence—
at ease.

1st

in the secrecy of defense
it was determined
initially approximately
to serve initially
training   conduct   defense

re-designated structure
special operations
combat support
service combat

internal communication
screens   assesses   selects
service tasked to train
scalable task in support
combatant internal defense

direct action
special deployment orders
six months then
continuously deployed

Traditions

coordinate them—

dress the baby and dog up as bees,
carve one pumpkin and leave the other intact,
hold the leash and push the stroller
around the block, a small parade

take snapshots of a toddling bee,
a bubble of stripes with blurry arms and legs

make a turkey dinner anyway,
yams, sprouts and red cabbage
for me and the baby, scraps for the dog,
eat leftovers for a week or more

keep the recipes to cook
an off-season Thanksgiving

hang stockings, bake pies,
the baby plays with red and gold paper
on Christmas Eve, she learns about gifts
and shares the paper with the dog

your stocking left hanging
and your gifts still wrapped

a timeline just slightly out of focus

Concerning Social Media

adequate protection
of critical information

vulnerabilities
tips to safeguard

proper security settings
limit visitors

you should keep to yourself
to a trusted circle

restricted access
personal information

guard
your identity

don't announce

where you are
where you've been

don't advertise
a pattern of life

exploitation of family
your home

make of car
street signs

remain vigilant
protect your family

you also protect
our people (yours)

Cemetery

nothing
only praise
proper tribute

those who lament
loss
mourn

of great history
of the greatest fight
piecemeal story of our dead

victory
cost
displaced ash

fortress
concrete
nearly victory

in doubt
whether any of us
in the end die knocking

crosses
count them
leave flowers

we wonder
who are our dead
the cost

side by side
names   ranks   rates
they are empty

A Funeral for Our Own

And there we were
all together for the first time
with one of us in an open casket
and a husband grieving for
the three months not shared.
Our hearts beat a cadence.
How little we help each other.
The life in slides looks like any
of us who smile for a camera,
hug near-strangers in times of public grief,
and in the end we embrace each other,
say *This is a sign, we need to be there*
but one honest wife says
with car keys in her hand
In the sixteen years
I have been married to the Corps,
this is the first time
I have gotten together with other wives.
I don't think it will happen again.

Penelope

The loom broke yesterday,
tired from its daily weaving,

so today I take the dog
on five long walks,

reorganize the kitchen
then put everything back

where it was before,
fix the loom

to fill this time of waiting.

Long Distance

When will you be home?
I wish I could say but I can't.
Two weeks between phone calls,
I have forgotten your voice.

I wish I could say but I can't
use the words that would say it all:
I have forgotten your voice,
and the baby does not know you.

I can't use the words that would say it all.
Two weeks between phone calls,
and the baby does not know you.
When will you be home?

Corps Value

New couponing class this Saturday,
no childcare provided.

You might qualify for WIC—
they provide formula and milk.

The thrift store is located next to
the Wounded Warrior rehab center.

Handouts can be difficult to accept.
It gets easier when you have kids.

Range Operations

High explosive munitions
rock the base
mortar   artillery—
at dusk Marines
beat a lullaby.

I prep my daughter's bath
call the night to order
sing *the ants go marching one by one*
as my dog curls up by my knees
and my baby calms.

Family Code

Your birthday month minus two,
our anniversary date divided by five,

plus the number of times

you went to the zoo without me,
minus the number of times

you walked the dog in the rain,

divided by the number of steps
you pace in the nursery,

plus the number of new words

our daughter says that aren't *da-da*,
and multiply it all by the miles

between us:

that is when I will retrograde,
but it could change.

III

*I wanted to know how it was to love somebody
the way Pop loved Mama. At least I wanted
a few days, or weeks if I could get it, to know
what it was like to be married. I wanted to be able
to say "I love you" a few times and mean it.*

—GySgt John Basilone, USMC

Deployment Coming to a Close

Your Marines and Sailors rejoin loved ones,
except those scheduled for schools and trainings.

After a long deployment, we know the value of family
so we apologize that the work days will be long.

The entire company will be home by mid-August,
but will not be granted the leave previously promised.

Please don't rely too heavily on our updates
as they change frequently.

*Don't expect your spouse to take over responsibilities
at home*, and be prepared for him to leave again.

It has been our honor to work with all the families.
We look forward to working with you again.

At Play

With their plastic knives and plastic guns,
the boys retreat from my yard—their shouts

of *We killed her! We killed her!*
move farther from me.

I collect the stones they tossed on the lawn,
heavy and cold in my hands.

The Amazons Prepare for Retrograde

We put our quivers and bows,
broadswords and shields

back in pantries behind reserves of

beans, rice and pasta.
Prop our feet on edges

of bathtubs to shave our legs,

whole cans of shave gel,
nicks around ankles and knees.

We paint our faces.

Shine our disguised armor:
necklaces and lockets, secure

them over our hearts
because we never know

what might hurl
through our doorways.

How Foolishly He Had Acted

All he wanted to do
when he came home

was turn on the TV,
then lie on the couch

and curve his back
to the screen and withdraw.

He didn't even want to eat,
but you kept insisting

going into great detail
about how many stores

before you found crème fraîche,
how you cut your finger

peeling potatoes, how you hated
chopping onions but diced four,

how you wanted this dinner

to be perfect,
how the tenderloin had to be marinated overnight

then braised for three hours,
how you made hot cross buns

from scratch and had to knead
the dough and let it rise,

then kneaded it again
and let it rise a little more

to show how much you missed him
to show him what he had missed.

Your love was designed to make him feel guilty.
And when you asked,

Are you at least going to help me wash dishes,
he knew it would just make you mad,

but he said *No*

Retrograde

Sharp bottle caps
litter the counter
keep company
with postcards
just now arriving
scrawled in familiar
penmanship
that forgot grammar
over time
over months.
Who is this
man who looks
somewhat like
the man who left,
somewhat thinner
somewhat darker
around the eyes?
The dog approaches
tail tucked
sniffs
bares teeth
retreats.

Group Meetings

a circle of folding chairs
a place to sit, to confess
what you may not be able to talk about—

get to know who we are:
preservation of force and families

later   the *I know your secrets* sidewise looks
at the exchange store,
We knew she couldn't handle it

offered once per month
appetizers will be served
you are welcome

Continued Operations

a family's support

belief in this battalion

let us return the standard

in atmosphere

in challenge and tasks

preparing for the retrograde

our partners

our fallen

after a 6-month job well done

unspoken award and honor

continued operations

a tempo for success

long days for the long-term

for the superb efforts

in this time

in this manner

we sustain a presence

we will miss them

A Dependable Order

I help you gather the pieces
of your dress blues

for the memorial service
of the fallen three—

you say you understand
why I choose to stay home.

I know what will happen—
the bugle will cry

the rifles will fire
family members will accept

Navy Crosses on behalf.
I sit in the quiet for an hour

then color-code the closet
alphabetize my books.

Posthumously

You will not wear these medals—
they are legacy and reminders. Yours
and not
yours. We want to thank you
for your sacrifice and ask

all who are witness
to this ceremony
to honor us with the same
dedication and willingness.

We would like to congratulate
all who will return to deployments.
You have set the standard
they will follow for success.

Widows Receive a Free Ticket
to the Birthday Ball

I.

Shadows of the fallen ones
crowd the black-draped table—
a single chair
for all who joined
one long history—
vigilant rose and flame,
sword and gloves at rest,
a purple heart for blood
shed.
Inverted place setting,
wine glass upside down,
silverware reversed,
they eat
in mirror to the living
lemon and salt of fate—

II.

Seated at a table of honor,
silk and rhinestones
no stiff wool jackets
no red striped trousers
the gold star spouses answer the roll call
for those who widowed them,
receive a standing ovation,
ooh-rahs and whistles.
They bow their heads
toward white linen,
pick at birthday cake.

III.

We sit in rings of couples
around our linen tables—
pass bread baskets, spread butter,
clink our glasses, complain about
small portions of beef and chicken.
We hold hands under tablecloths
wishing we could kiss
the one beside for once.
Maybe we will dance.
Maybe we will retire early.

3rd Anniversary

our first together
and we don't know
what to do for
occasions like these

Words from Friends

I'd look forward to
months to myself,
doing my own thing.

My husband is gone a lot, too—
he works over 50 hours a week.

You get military discounts—
you should be happy.

It's been two weeks
since you heard from him?
Aren't you worried?

The news said
5 Marines were killed today.

Doesn't your husband miss
seeing your daughter grow up?

If your husband cared
about his family,
he'd get a different job.

This is what you chose.

Irregular

Some said *They rode in*
on their high horses,
grabbing women
as they swaggered by.

Some said *I saw them*
swing lefts and rights
into every eye socket
inside and outside
every Oceanside bar.

Some said *Our home*
values will lower
now that they returned
to our community.

But I saw one of them,
and he refused to talk
about what he'd done
or where he'd been.
He slept every day past noon.

Between Trainings and Deployments

She asks,
Are you having fun?
You've been pushing
your daughter on the swing/
playing catch/
(insert happy father activity)
and you haven't smiled yet.
We're at the Redwoods/
at the natural history museum/
(insert family vacation)
can you at least pretend to have fun?
Are you angry?
Are you tired?
Are you happy?

He says,
I'm fine.

Brides and Grooms

this life will
mould you flat

shove you into tiny spaces
carved from tradition

extra medals and ranks
with earrings and bracelets

side by side
at balls, holiday parties

side by side
through moto speeches

packing and unpacking
suitcases, boxes

some boxes
never unpacked

but there's this:
you are meant to be at odds

the pretty good
hang onto that

when this life is over

you'll want that person again

the good enough
the real

Your eyes
in the shadow
of your cover.

Notes on the Poems

LtGen Lewis B. "Chesty" Puller, USMC: He served from 1918-1955. He fought and led through battles in the Banana Wars, World War II and the Korean War. Puller is the only Marine to have been awarded five Navy Crosses. He retired after suffering a stroke.

Wedding Arch: The original Mameluke Blade was a sword presented by Prince Hamet of the Ottoman Empire to 1stLt Presley O'Bannon as gratitude for his Marines' service in the Battle of Tripoli. Replicas of this sword are carried by officers. It is used in ceremonies, such as the Marine Corps Birthday Ball, graduations, funerals, and weddings. Marines stand in two lines with the swords raised to form an arch.

Unconventional Warfare: A moto wife lives, breathes and sweats Marine Corps. She is always supportive and accepting.

Lejeune's Resolution: LtGen John A. Lejeune, USMC, served from 1890-1929 and is nicknamed "The Marine's Marine." He fought and led through the Spanish-American War, the Philippine-American War, the Mexican Revolution, and World War I, and he served as the 13th Commandant of the Marine Corps. While Commandant, he gave his famous address on 1 November, 1921 in commemoration of the Marine Corps Birthday. His resolution is printed and read as part of the ceremonies of every successive Birthday Ball.

Esprit de Corps at Home: Some words are borrowed and altered from President Harry S. Truman's September 1950 letter *The Marine Corps as the Navy's Police Force*.

Watching the Birthday Moto Video: At each Marine Corps Birthday Ball, a motivational video is shown.

Uniform: A cover is a hat that is worn as part of a uniform. A different cover is required for utility, service and dress. Some words are borrowed and altered from Gen David M. Shoup's, USMC, 4 January 1960 remarks on the *Swagger Stick*.

SgtMaj Daniel J. "Dan" Daley, USMC: He served from 1899-1929. He fought and led through the Boxer Rebellion, the Banana Wars and World War I and is one of seven Marines to have received that Medal of Honor twice. He gave his famous battle cry during the Battle of Belleau Wood, World War I.

For Efficiency: The words "kindly and just" are the title of a 19 September 1922 letter by MajGen John A. Lejeune, USMC.

Family Readiness: Family Readiness Folders are put together before deployments. Because Marines cannot easily be reached during deployments to provide information or answer questions, the folders serve as reference to help with banking issues or such. They also contain information needed in the case of death in service.

Law: Some words are borrowed and altered from *An Act for Establishing and Organizing a Marine Corps*, U.S. Congress, 11 July 1798.

Geometry of Fire on the Local News: Geometry of fire is a term used for battlefield geometry that involves ammunition. While three fires at Camp Pendleton burned nearly 22,000 acres on 13 May, 2013, Marines continued to train.

The Pit Opened Up: erasures from Book Revelations in *The Holy Bible*, *The Utility of Force: The Art of War in the* Modern World by General Rupert Smith, and *Cars and Trucks and Things that Go* by Richard Scarry

Cemetery: Some words are borrowed and altered from the *Dedication of the 3d Marine Division Cemetery* speech by MajGen Graves B. Erskine, USMC, February 1945.

Family Code: Retrograde is the term used for moving away from the battle. It is used when the servicemen leave the deployment duty to return home. It is a security risk to make public, voice in phone calls or write in emails the dates of travel and return.

GySgt John Basilone, USMC: He served in the United States Army from 1936-1939 and in the Marine Corps from 1940-1945. He was awarded the Medal of Honor for his bravery in the Battle of Guadalcanal, World War II. After receiving the Medal of Honor, he began war bond tours in 1943. He could have continued these tours, but wanted to return to action. He petitioned to return to active duty, and was sent to train at Camp Pendleton where he fell in love with and married a female Marine. Soon after the honeymoon, he requested to return to the fighting in the Pacific. He died in action on the first day of the Battle of Iwo Jima. He was posthumously awarded the Navy Cross.

A Dependable Order: The dress blues is the uniform for special events: balls, weddings, funerals, and posthumous award ceremonies.

Posthumously: Ceremonies are given for those who are awarded medals and other honors after death in service. Spouses, parents or others accept awards and medals for actions in battle; the battalion attends.

Widows Receive a Free Ticket to the Birthday Ball: The black table for those who have fallen in service is part of the ceremonies of every Marine Corps Birthday Ball. Gold star spouses is the term used for those widowed in sacrifice and service to the nation.

About the Author

Lisa Stice received a BA in English literature from Mesa State College (now Colorado Mesa University) and an MFA in creative writing and literary arts from the University of Alaska Anchorage. She taught high school for ten years and is now a military wife who lives in North Carolina with her husband, daughter and dog. You can find out more about her and her publications at:

lisastice.wordpress.com and facebook.com/LisaSticePoet